QED START Maths

Sizes and Shapes

Book 1

Ann Montague-Smith

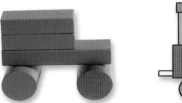

QED Publishing

First published in the UK in 2004 by
QED Publishing
A division of Quarto Publishing plc
The Fitzpatrick Building
188-194 York Way, London N7 9QP

A Catalogue record for this book is available from the British Library.

ISBN 1-84538-026-6

Written by Ann Montague-Smith
Designed and edited by The Complete Works
Illustrated by Jenny Tulip
Photography by Steve Lumb and Michael Wicks

Creative Director Louise Morley
Editorial Manager Jean Coppendale

Printed and bound in China

With thanks to:

Contents

Cubes and spheres

Point to the cubes.

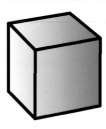

cube

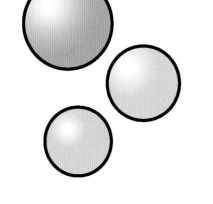

Point to the spheres.

sphere

Challenge
Find some building blocks. Sort out the cubes. Now sort out the spheres.

5

Pyramids and cones

Point to the cones.

cone

Use some pyramid and cone building bricks.
Make some more trees for the picture.

6

Point to the pyramids.

pyramid

Challenge
Find some cubes, spheres, cones and pyramids. Make a house for the picture. Which shapes are good for building? Why do you think that?

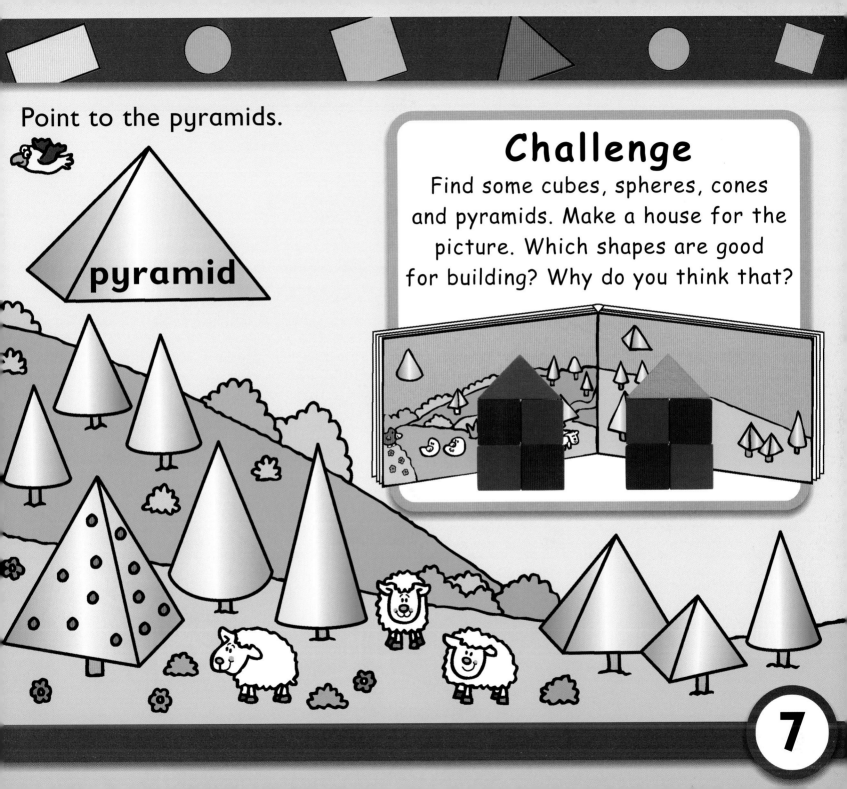

Shape match

Match the shapes that are the same.

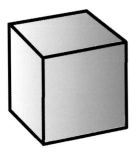
cube

sphere

cone

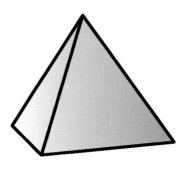
pyramid

8

Say the names of the shapes.

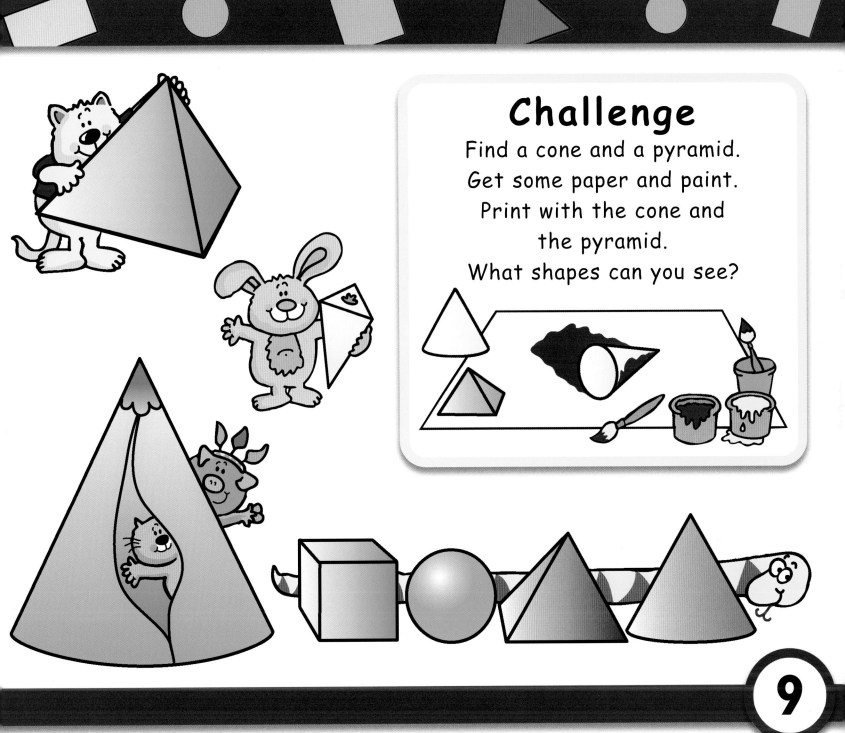

Challenge

Find a cone and a pyramid.
Get some paper and paint.
Print with the cone and
the pyramid.
What shapes can you see?

Squares and circles

You will need some red and blue counters.
Put a red counter on each square.

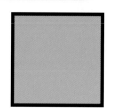 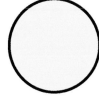

square **circle**

Put a blue counter on each circle.

10

Challenge

Use coloured gummed paper squares and circles. Make your own people from these shapes.

11

Triangles and rectangles

Point to the triangles.

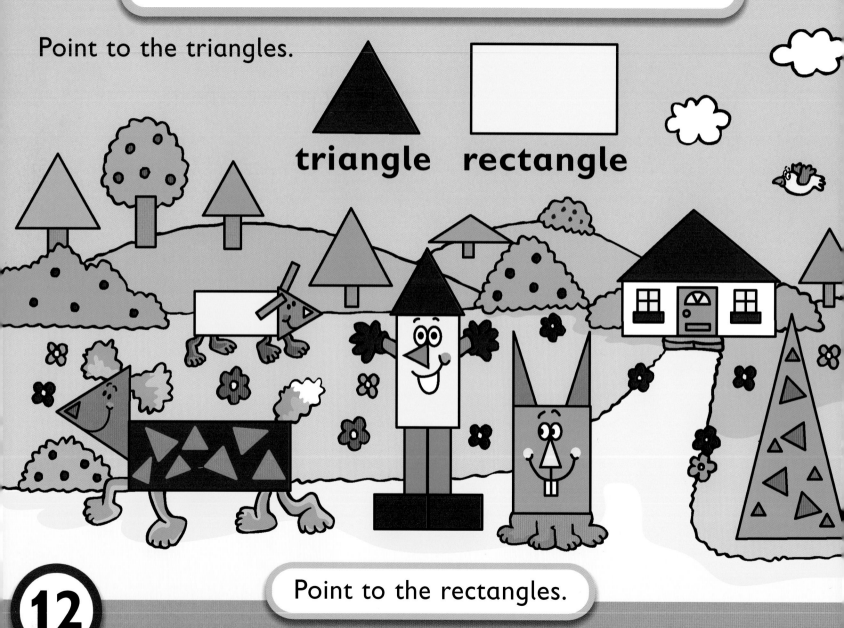

triangle   rectangle

Point to the rectangles.

12

Challenge

Find some triangle and rectangle flat shapes. Make your own animals with these shapes.

Make a picture

You will need some square, rectangle, triangle and circle flat shapes. Use the shapes to make the pictures.

Which shapes did you use to make your pictures?

Challenge

Make your own picture using squares, rectangles, triangles and circles.

Up and down

Two of you play this game with 3 counters. Take turns to throw a counter onto the spinner. Move your counter to the next square with the spinner shape on it. Move up a ladder and down a hose. The winner is the first one to reach the finish.

start

finish

Challenge

Find a friend, a doll's house and a toy chair. Ask your friend to shut their eyes. Put the chair in the doll's house and say where it is. Ask your friend to open their eyes. Can they find the chair?

17

Where is it?

Point to the top of the climbing frame.

What is at the bottom of the slide?

Where would you like to play?

What would you do?

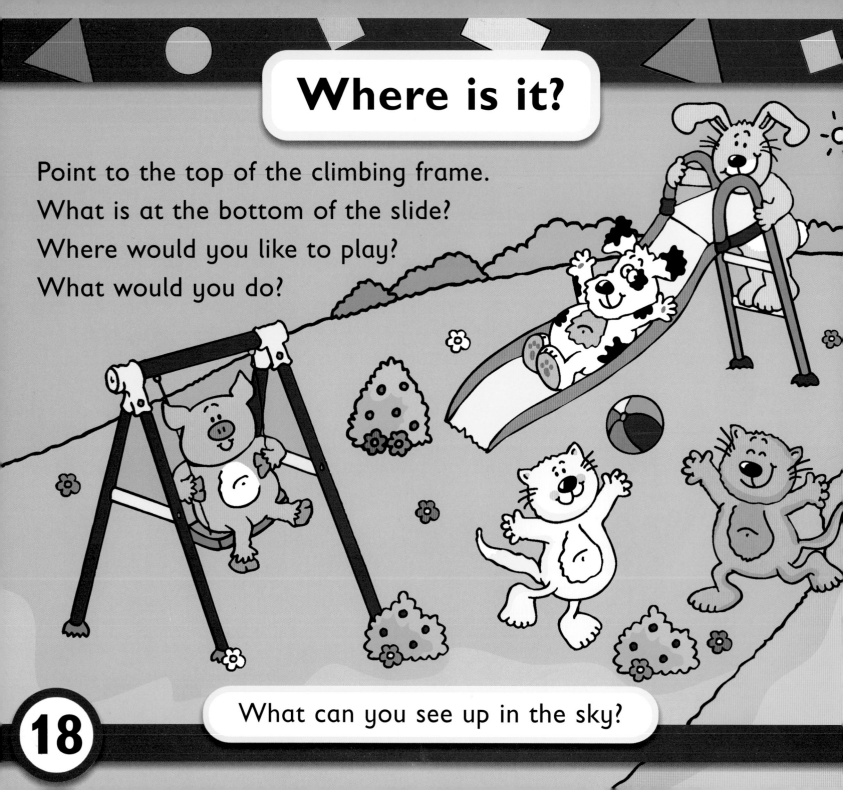

What can you see up in the sky?

Challenge

Play 'I Spy' with a friend.
Look around you.
Say, 'I spy something on
top of the cupboard.'

Ask your friend to guess what
the object is. When your
friend has answered you, it's
then your friend's turn
to have a go.

19

Get some counters. Listen to the word.
Put a counter on the picture that matches the word.

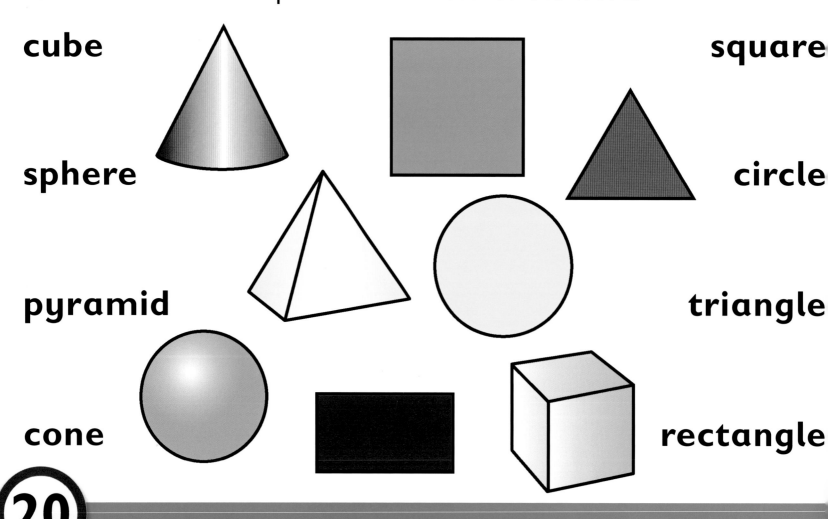

cube

sphere

pyramid

cone

square

circle

triangle

rectangle

20

on top

underneath

up

down

Challenge
Look around you.
Can you find the shapes on these pages?
Now look for things that are up or down.
Can you find things that are
on top or underneath?

21

Supporting notes for adults

Cubes and spheres – pages 4-5

At this stage, children may call these shapes 'box' and 'ball'.
Practise together saying 'cube' and 'sphere'.

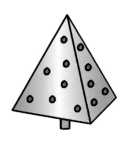

Pyramids and cones – pages 6-7

If children are unsure about cones, talk about ice-cream cones. Similarly, there is
a chocolate which comes in a pyramid-shaped box. Discuss this with the children.

Shape match – pages 8-9

Encourage the children to say the names of the shapes that they see in the picture.
Ask questions such as, 'What is the same shape? What is different about these shapes?'

Squares and circles–pages 10-11

Point to the shapes at the top of the pages and say their names: 'circle… square.'
Ask the children to practise saying these words.

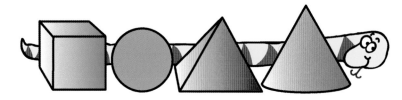

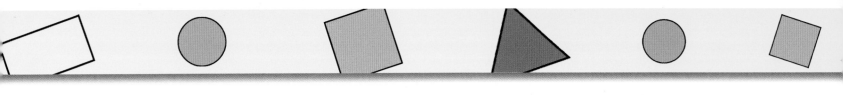

Triangles and rectangles – pages 12-13

Again, practise saying the names of these shapes. Children may confuse squares and rectangles. Provide some rectangle and square flat shapes for the children to sort, so that they begin to recognize the similarities and differences.

Make a picture – pages 14-15

If the children find it difficult to make the pictures using shapes, ask them to show you each shape in turn, for one of the pictures. Together, use these shapes to make the picture.

Up and down – pages 16-17

Talk about 'up' and 'down'. If children are unsure, ask them to stretch up, then squat down. As the children play the game ask, 'Which way will you move now? Up or down?'

Where is it? – pages 18-19

Ask questions about the picture, using words such as high, low, beside, behind, on top, under... Encourage the children to say what they can see in these positions.

I know – pages 20-21

Read the shape words. Ask the children to say which shape word describes which picture. Some of the pictures will have 2 ideas, such as up and down. Encourage the children to show you which part of the picture depicts each idea.

Suggestions for using this book

Children will enjoy looking through the book and talking about the colourful pictures. Sit somewhere comfortable together. Please read the instructions to the children, then encourage them to take part in the activity and check whether or not they have understood what to do.

In this book, children are introduced to the solid shapes of cubes, spheres, pyramids and cones. Please encourage them to sort out building blocks to find examples of these shapes. At first they may call a cube a 'box', a sphere a 'ball'. This is quite acceptable and shows that they are recognizing these mathematical shapes in everyday things.

The flat shapes introduced are squares, circles, triangles and rectangles. Encourage children to recognize that squares are the faces of cubes, that pyramids have triangular faces, and so on. This will help to avoid confusion later on in their learning between which are solid and which are flat shapes.

Encourage the children to talk about the properties of shapes, such as which solid shapes have flat faces, and which curved. This will help them to distinguish the shapes.

Children will enjoy making their own models and pictures from shapes, as well as copying the ones given in the book. Encourage them to talk about which shapes would be good to make something, and why that is so.

When the children tackle each Challenge, ask questions such as, 'Why do you think that? Is there another way to do this? What else could you try?'